HOME FREE

POEMS BY APARNA PAUL

HOME FREE

Cover art by Catherine Weiss.

Edited by Myles Taylor.

www.gameoverbooks.com

EVERYONE LOVES A PARTY
after "Variations on a Theme by Elizabeth Bishop" by John Murillo

lose everything. lose your closest friendships while trying to plan a party. lose your sense of self in the Costco bakery section. lose your car in the Party City parking lot. lose an entire afternoon in traffic. lose your way home; but remember: we only feel homesick when we're gone. remember: you didn't know what home felt like until you left. remember: you lost your mom in the parking lot. you lost your voice yelling her name. you lost your innocence when you found out your mom's name isn't Mom. you lost it again when you find out she never wanted to be called Mom, she wanted to be called Mummy, which is what she calls her mom. in the end everyone calls for their mother. lose your whole history in a single syllable. lose your cool. lose it, i'm serious. cool is overrated. lose an enemy and invite them to the party instead. lose out on every other party happening on Saturday night. lose track of how many shots you had; have another. lose track of how many shots you had; have another. lose track——————————————————. lose a whole hour of your life and ply your friends in the morning to give it back. they will remember, and you will think you do, too. will remember the outlines of it even as you lose trust in the details. lose your ex's number, why do you even have that. lose your keys. lose your breath on the dance floor. lose your way back to the kitchen. did you lose your keys? it doesn't matter, it's your house. lose your grip on the cake. lose a whole cake. lose your appetite when you look at the cake on the floor. lose your grip on the situation. lose control. control is overrated. lose your voice, again. lose your cool. lose your breath. lose it, and go outside to breathe in deep. lose the angry red air from your lungs. lose your lungs. lose your body. remember your body. you can only remember something once it's lost. you can only lose something once it's remembered, fuzzy outline but no trust. lose the details. lose the outline. lose your way back in; where the fuck are your keys; there's no one left at the party. lose yourself in the night sky, in the way your breath steams in the dark, every loss
inside of you
trying to get found
out.

these days, everybody wants to hear the prophecies of yore at a mcdonald's drive thru, and i just don't think that's what i'm after

& when my friend pulls up & the speaker starts crackling with some eldritch horror,
     & it asks, *do you want to die with that?*
& my friend looks over at me & asks, *well, do you?*
& i say *i'm good with just the pepsi, thanks*
& the eldritch horror, profound & decrepit, wails like a thousand suns being
     born or the edge of a paper slicing through skin or your dad shutting
     the door on your family the morning that he dies
& my friend says, oh, *i think they only have coke products here,*
& i say, *hm, then i guess a cherry coke*
& my friend says, *okay, a mcchicken, a cherry coke, plus can i get an answer to the*
     question unspoken in my heart? because my friend is always saying shit
     like that, especially in the mcdonald's drive thru
& this time the voice from the speaker is sweet dulcet caramel dripping off a
     spoon, a siren song in symphony,
& my friend says, *damn, i think i'm a dollar short,*
     but it's okay because i have two dollars in my pocket, & anyway, the
     prophecies are free here, free like the way any of us are, free as a man
     with an albatross around his neck, free as an albatross around a man's
     neck, since the albatross is dead, and isn't death a kind of freedom?,
     free like a limited time only BOGO sale at the Gap, free like you'll still
     have to give up your firstborn son, but whatever, who's having
     babies in this economy, anyway, not to mention your firstborn
     won't be a sun, if anything they'll be the MOON,
& we drive to the window
& my friend's camry sounds like it might fall apart right there
& so might i, if i'm being honest
& i look into the black hole at the first window
     or rather, it looks into me,
     i blink first
& it becomes a murder of crows, silent, except to say
     second window only tonight,
& we're at the second window,
     which is a little grimy,
     with a freckled bespectacled teen behind it,
& she looks like me, a study in personal time travel,
     but when i ask my friend he says, *hey, doesn't that guy look like me?*

so it could be the whole world, or nothing at all
& i'm handed the cherry coke without much fanfare
& the teen leans out the window to whisper in my friend's ear
& i strain to listen
        but all i hear is the rustling of the first breeze that ever swept this earth,
& when my friend turns to me,
        he says, *prophecy machine is down tonight. can i get a sip of your cherry coke?*
& we drive away, dial-shifting through static,
        as the world dissolves into whipping wind, fresh fizz,
& our laughter, spilling into empty eternity

what follows is a series of lies my mom refused to tell me

Santa Claus is real,

unseasoned broccoli tastes good,

you'll live forever,

I'll live forever,

everything will be OK,

yes, you should get bangs,

the color grey looks good on you,

the medical industrial complex in this country will protect you,

having children was the best thing that ever happened to me,

always follow expiration dates on food,

we are required to love and forgive the people who have hurt us,

we are required to love and forgive the people who have hurt us

        simply because they are family,

homemade brownies taste better than Ghirardelli box mix,

we'll always have our memories,

yes, you're good at playing tennis,

yeah, I made that biryani too spicy,

2% milk is the same thing as whole milk,

whole wheat bread tastes better than white bread,

you should force yourself through something you're not enjoying,

I love you, too,

you can do it on your own, without me,

you can walk through this world with your eyes closed.

& every time I kissed someone for the first time

it was like every first kiss I'd ever had,
a slow-rolling train of accumulation, slick lubricant memory on the tracks

& when our friends shrieked with joy in the next room
& when he leaned down in the neon pink residue glow
& when he said *I don't know how, but I have to tell you something*
I wasn't there

& when the sitcom kept rolling in the background, laughter of the dead
& when she said *I love the way you laugh*
& when she leaned in close
I wasn't there

& when "Toxic" by Britney Spears blew out my eardrums
& when her voice cut through it—ringing, sharp, true—
& when she said *I just want you to know*
I wasn't there

& in the Taco Bell drive thru at midnight
& in the library stacks between Vonnegut + Wilkerson
& by the bike racks in the summer
& while I held a guitar + a mug of wine + her hand + his shirt + everything + nothing
I wasn't there

& every time i kissed someone for the first time
my mind fractured like a mirror
eleven years of bad luck later
a memory I couldn't forget
where was I / where was I
a mouth on mine
cold + gray + clammy + a witness to the dead, to the breath leaving my body
nothing pressing me down except the weight of the whole world

when I said I couldn't stand being alone
that's what I mean
I wasn't standing
I was on my back
someone else was there

but I was alone
in my own mind
it was breaking
in the way that a plate does
or trust
or a family

or maybe not breaking
but a mouth opening
lips parting,

if something enters you
something else must leave

but everything here
is still here

& I wasn't there, either
I wasn't anywhere

except I was on the tip of a tongue
myself a memory I couldn't remember

olden shovel with a voicemail from my mom

what the fuck was up with that? when i told my dad that story he said, aw he's trying, and my *mom*
laughed in response, she knows that *here,*
trying looks a lot like taunting, *just*
like a melting pot looks like slow death by fire, she *saw*
how some people don't have tongues, they have mirrors, & i knew that
i don't have a tongue, i have a black hole, so when *you*
said that to me, the word namaste *had*
disappeared down the gullet like a fish *called*
back to sea, swallowed *so*
fast i wondered at my own lips, never forming hello but always forming *i'm*
sorry, for not being enough, for being too much, for not having the right words, or the right language, for *calling*
across the void & hoping to hear only echo *back*
no one in my family says namaste because there's enough body language to know a homecoming at first glance,
in the mirror, at the kitchen table, they're all the same anyway; me and my reflection,
we're not alone here, i've got my dad's eyes and my mom's smile but *actually*
these laugh lines belong to my *nani*
somehow stitching the whole world together *and*
still having a hand free to beat us at cards, *i*
lost but i didn't mind, it was better than losing my mind, most things *are*
my mind my memory my meal all of us around the table, *sitting*
in eager anticipation for the next deal or the next dinner, and wouldn't you believe i'm not a particularly good indian
in that i'm rarely writing about the heritage home cooking
but i'm a great american in that i'm almost always writing about arriving *at*
yet another fast food chain, salvation in the *wendy's*
drive through if i look hard enough if i let myself admit what's *eating*
me alive: that i didn't mind that much when you said namaste, that i was more *chicken*
to the fact that it was a word that never comes from my own mouth, those syllables, precious *nuggets*
of truth bursting forth on your tongue unraveling words, worlds, isn't it enough to know we want to *talk*
to one another? isn't it enough *to*
hope that *you*
& i might look past tongues, or language, find only heart, *later*

i spell my name

for a barista and halfway through
i forget what i am doing
i stand there / in silence
she stares at me
did i forget my name
did i forget how to name myself
did i forget / myself / and
can i call it forgetting
if it felt like / relief

in my dream / i consider changing my name / to all names
i imagine the name that is easier to pronounce than the one i have
and the name that is harder to pronounce than the one i have
i imagine the name of the past / my mother's or my father's
i imagine the name of the future / the name of the sun that will rise tomorrow

in my mom's religion a child is not given a name until their seventh day
in my childhood my father asked me not to name my mother's religion
when i asked why / his response was not
that it was three years after nine eleven
and we had moved to the most conservative county in america
he didn't have to say that part
he just said my name

aparna means without leaves
i had to google that because strangers kept asking me what my name meant
when i asked my parents the same question
they just said we don't know we just liked how it sounded have you tried googling it

my parents, of different religions, did not choose
a name in either one at risk of offending the other's family / instead
chose a name that meant nothing
aparna means without leaves / barren
wasteland brought to bear
no leaves on the family tree
empty / empty
a man speaks urdu to me and before i can respond

my friend says *she doesn't speak urdu / she doesn't speak / anything*
nothing Nothing nothing
the silence / may as well be my name
empty / everywhere

so why i ask
i am always asking why / useless pursuit of meaning
WHY did you choose this name
my parents say
because we liked the director Aparna Sen
because i hear / i am always listening for the because
BECAUSE we heard a name / and saw a storyteller
because Because because
we heard a name that meant / empty
because when there are no leaves / there are no leaves yet
and that means anything / anything
might bloom

ode to the drunk girl at the party crying into the sink

we don't love her because she's drunk. we don't love her because she's telling us about her ex. we don't love her because she wants to call him. we don't love her because we're stumbling back to the kitchen, her phone just out of reach of her sticky fingers. we don't love her because she's tossing back that next shot. we don't love her because she's trying to forget and instead all she gets more remember. we tell her he's a bastard, an asshole. we tell her she's better. we tell her she could do better. we tell her she'd better, next time. we want what she wants. she wants what we want. what do we want? the world to keep spinning. someone, even someone far away, to think of us, for however brief a moment, to think of how our hair looked in the morning right before we woke up, to think of an errant dried crust of sleep along our eyelids, because we slept so deeply, because we knew we were safe. we love her because we love her because we love her because we don't know how to do anything else.

i don't remember the movie but i remember in it a character dies

& as he lays dying he says:
i want to go home
& *i want to go home* but:
i don't know what that means
because when i was in high school
       i stayed as far away from the house for as long as possible
because when i ate dinner at the kitchen table
       i stared at the clock to make the numbers turn faster
because when i was in college
       there was a month i called my parents every day and my mom would
       never say *i love you* but she would always ask *what did you have for dinner?*
because when i asked my mom how long she was homesick after moving to this country
       she said *i still am*

so now when i say the word home,
i say it as though it is mukhwas,
fennel seeds & anise & rose leaves,
sugared sweet, hard on the teeth,
yes, i say the word home like it's mukhwas,
like it's dissolving on my tongue, like it's
bright & cold & gone
but still in my gums four hours later,
my mouth open in the moonlight

see i want to go home but:
i stay too late at parties / i keep everyone up worrying / especially myself
until reluctantly:
the sorry sidewalk stumble
to the place i cannot name
my feet carry me to this doormat & that leaky radiator & those umbrellas,
       drying on the rack
& my feet could've carried me anywhere
they could've brought me to the edge of the map
where the borders warp & tear
or they could've walked me to the center of the earth
furnace flames searing shoes so
the ground could kiss my soles
but instead they've brought me here,
home free, but does that mean i'm free to go home, or that i'm free of a home?
is freedom having a place to go / or not?

as he lay dying:
he said:
i want to go home
& i want to go home
but i don't know what that means
& i don't know, when i lay dying, what i will say
but if i said that
& if my mother heard
she would slap me into the next life anyway:
she would say:
not know what home means? did i not teach you this language?
did i not give it to you from my own tongue?
she would say: was this home not enough for you?
was this hot meal not a hearth?
was this house not four walls that kept rain off your head?
she would say: have this dinner. you'll be alright after dinner.
she would say: have this mukhwas. let your mouth be clean of wishes,
let the only dreams be in your sleep.
she would say: i want to go home, too:

**thought to be one of the rarest snakes in north america, no louisi-
ana pine snake has been seen in the last decade, until today, when
we start to see them everywhere**

there are only sixteen louisiana pine snakes in the world & we begin to notice;
the remaining snakes all grow to outrageous sizes, the height of the eiffel tower,
swaddling the statue of liberty as though giving her a scarf, draped over the
washington monument like an errant garden hose over a patio chair. the us
military does what they usually do when faced with a problem they don't entirely
understand, bombing a snake switchbacking the great smoky mountains, which
means:

there are only fifteen louisiana pine snakes in the world & they all grow larger;
an absence doubling the amount of space the rest of them take up, grief blooming
big enough so we have no choice but to / remember.

there are only nine louisiana pine snakes in the world & they demand to be
known;
one stretches across the chesapeake bay, displacing the bridge, across new england,
rhode island is obliterated, none in death valley, that's too much foreshadowing
for an endangered species / one wraps round & round west virginia, no country
roads to take any of us home.

there are only seven louisiana pine snakes in the world & they bring us closer to
one another;
they reach across oceans, bering strait land bridge restored 11000 years later, &
across continents, silk road made living, made slithering / a sister stands on one
side, hand pressed to scaled division, & on the other, her brother imagines he can
feel her heartbeat, or is that the snake's? it's all the same.

there are only three louisiana pine snakes in the world & they're visible from
everywhere on the planet;
a man in brazil stands shadowed by gaping maw, tooth size of everest, a woman
in turkey beholds its tail / everyone witnessing the same miracle even / if no one
has the words for it.

there is only one louisiana pine snake & it is the world;
it wraps around the globe / eternal squeeze it unhinges its jaw / it swallows us
whole / keeps on swallowing / tongue tail body disappeared down the throat / all
of us inside, forever, falling into the truth of ourselves

burning

in a high school
in south central pennsylvania summer
tennis coach barbara tells us
to wear sunscreen, says
it's the most important protection

the sun glares down onto us
on the court where we all
        stand   like   outstretched   fingers
                reaching to the clouds in the sky

barbara is wearing
a wide-brimmed hat &
long sleeves &
sunglasses &
her nose is caked in spf 70 &

when someone asks her
why she's so adamant on us using sunscreen
she talks about
        her childhood in arizona
                toasted beyond tan
                adolescence burnt to a crisp

she says
back in my day
it was cool
to be this
        dark
like
        darker than aparna

did you forget
i was in this story?
did you picture
a high school in south central pennsylvania summer &
imagine only

white clouds &
white sun &
white streak of spf 70 &
white lines on the tennis court &

white

space

                          with only nothingness between?

it's ok
if you did.
i grew up in that
              place. i know what it's like
                         to forget my own existence
                                     even when i'm standing
right here

nothing as dark as
         a shadow of myself, shrinking in the sun
         closed eyes refusing to see
         the mark on the ruler, person made unit of measurement & nothing
else
         whatever is left after the sun goes supernova,
                white   hot intensity,
                       burning the whole world,
consuming everything here that has color,
                                    texture,
                                    life—

it's okay, barbara
i get
         your analogy

at the end of the summer,
         your tan would fade
               make you   white again

at the end of your sentence,

         you skin me alive

                 no more   brown

just

white

bones

with nothing

in between.

I DREAM MY MOTHER ON HER DEATHBED &

it's a dream i've had before
in the way that i am a child
that my mother has had before
in the way that both
are nightmares

& when was the last time
i looked at my mother?
when was the last time i saw her
for who she was & not
for what my memory made her?

my memory made her
      tall
          & glamorous
    & angry
                        & intimidating
      & loving
             & gentle
                    & clicking her tongue
    & home style haircuts
            & laughing too loudly
               & earrings that go
               clink

but i find in this place
that if memory has made her all those things then
unmemory has made her
      hair against the pillow &
      wretched at the lips &
      she's shorter than i am, but
      i don't remember
      when that happened, &
      they won't let her wear earrings here &
      glamorous,
      i promise, no mom, i'm not just saying it to make you happy, i really
          think that &
maybe it's cruel to ask so much of memory when she no longer has hers

I DREAM MY MOTHER ON HER DEATHBED &
she once told me
she was ready to die
because she had done
everything she wanted to in life &
she was 53 when she said that
but i guess when she said that
i was 17 &
i was ready to die too

I DREAM MY MOTHER ON HER DEATHBED &
the last time we had a conversation,
a real conversation,
we were
on the phone & we were arguing
about something stupid &
i don't remember
what & a woman overheard me on the street &
                              she said are you ok? &
        i said yeah it's just my mom &
                              the woman said oh
                              i know that conversation &
she was a stranger on the street
but if she had asked
what are you fighting about
        i would have responded:
the same thing
all mothers & daughters fight about:
                              how to survive

I DREAM MY MOTHER ON HER DEATHBED &
when i was born

                                        i nearly killed her
when she had me

                                        i almost died
& our two lives have been one
                    slow
                    suicide pact
                                        ever since

MY MOTHER DREAMT ME ON MY DEATHBED &

i survived

I DREAM MY MOTHER ON HER DEATHBED &

she doesn't

I DREAM MY MOTHER
ON HER DEATHBED &

MY MOTHER DREAMS ME
ON MY DEATHBED &

I DREAM OUR
DEATHBEDS ARE THE SAME &

OUR HOUSES WERE
THE SAME ONCE &

OUR BODIES WERE
THE SAME ONCE &

OUR MEMORIES MAY NEVER
EVER BE THE SAME AGAIN BUT

IS IT SO EXTRAORDINARY TO IMAGINE
THAT OUR DREAMS WON'T BE DIFFERENT?

i dream my mother on her deathbed
& it's a dream
i've always had
& always will have

        a reassurance

because it is easier to have
this dream
than to have
this world
without her

ekphrasis after the moderated panel on the exhibition Please Stay Home at Harvard's Carpenter Center, free to all, featuring the work of Darrel Ellis, who died of AIDS in 1992

He was told that the inkwashes he was doing were not innovative enough.
He wanted to make bigger art.
He reflected.
He was very poetic.
He felt like an outsider.
He was a classically figurative painter.
He was interested in the figure in a way that was away from others.
He sat for Hujar to shoot him.
He was shot.
He created a painting afterwards.
He saw everything.
He paid homage to the past.
He was transforming his present.

His past is transforming him.

He wrought activity from the shadows *the blacks are alive.*
He has created a body of work with contingencies, seriality.

He resists the canon.

He created *Untitled (Laure on Easter Sunday).*
He is exploding a sense of materiality into the object.
He is proving to us what we thought was experimental is just the start.
He is representative of the city.

He was not representative of the city.
He was the archive.

He is the ghost in the machine.
He is the ghost.
He is superhuman.
He is more than a mind.
He doesn't mind.
He is just a body, after all.
He brings the work to life.
He captures the liveliness of the scene.

He lived.

He is dead.
He is a story with a million threads waiting to be pulled.

He was a man but now he is a ball of yarn.
He transformed his present so much that, we regret to inform you,
he's no longer with us.

He transformed his present so much that, we regret to inform you,

                    he's no longer with us.

He didn't die; he transformed.
He transformed into HIV positive.
He transformed into AIDS patient.
He transformed into a body.
He was, you know.
He was possessed by the past.
He used photos.
He remembered someone else's memories.
He disappeared into the work.

                    He is in the negatives.
            He's just in the dark room, shall I fetch him.

He didn't make prints of his father's work.
He made contact sheets.

                    He has a father.

He did not meet his father.
He had a father.

                He reacts against the father.
         He uses his father's art as a beginning.

He used his father's art as an end.
He began.

                    He ends.

He does not destroy;

                he regenerates.

He was methodical.
He took photographs.
He wasn't interested in photography.
He made plaster reliefs.
He used bandages.
He had to do everything in a makeshift way.
He took photographs.
He sculpted.
He painted.
He created.
He was fascinated by the possibilities.
He dreamt. He dreamt. He dreamt.

                    He dreams.

elegy for who i was yesterday

after Jade Kleiner

i ate a klondike bar
standing over the kitchen sink

the chocolate left impressions in the grooves of my fingerprints
or my fingers left impressions in the hard shell

either way both things were softer
than i had previously imagined

the ice cream ran rivulets down my wrists
it was too late for a bowl

it's almost always too late to know what to do with the overflow
besides let it pass through your fingers

surrender to the stainless steel
the sink perfect cemetery of the things that served us so well

that will serve us again
so long as we muster the courage to indulge

our slacker sabbath but til then i'll be holy water
cleansed with melting vanilla

made sweeter by the wreckage in my own hands
made fuller by the things that were frozen once

but which melt into myself
made mere memory

of sitting on a couch somewhere far away
kicking my legs against the air

my brother & my mom both saying how
did you get ice cream on your elbow of all places

remembering i have an elbow of all things
& realizing that my tongue, no matter what shape it made

could never reach the point
maybe we don't reach it but

reach towards it forever like a promise
like a prayer like pursuit of perfection

& we never get there
but we still keep going

man lies

wait let me start over

man climbs banana tree
man falls from banana tree
man lies
in dirt
man stares at sky
sky tessellates
through tree tremors
man says, to no one,
i have never
seen a day
more beautiful
than this one
man lies
wait let me start over

man sits on airplane for 14 hours
man gets off airplane
man has never been so happy
to see dirt
man lies
in dirt
someone says, to him,
     hey, man, that's my yard,
     get the fuck out
man says, to no one,
     how can someone own
     dirt? it's dirt

     man moves into apartment
dirt moves into apartment
     man sweeps
dirt moves into apartment
     man sweeps
dirt moves into apartment
     man
applies for green card

         man
is denied green card
why's it even called a green card
dirt moves into apartment
          man sweeps
dirt into garbage bag
garbage bag is green / green is garbage bag
man, i don't want this

green card. this country is garbage
man, many years in the future, says, to me,
there is no piece of paper more powerful than the us passport,
except, for maybe, the us dollar,
man lies
wait let me start over

man sits at dinner table
kids kick each other under dinner table
man says, to them,
          if you don't
          finish your food,
          a tiger will eat
          your dinner & then
          eat you
man says, to them,
          i should know,
          it happened to me once,
          a tiger chased me
          up a banana tree
          i climbed & climbed & climbed until i forgot
          to be afraid
man lies
wait let me start over

daughter says, to man,
          look, i drew this for you
man says, to daughter,
          oh…what is it?

daughter says, to man,
          it's a banana tree
man looks at drawing
how could any piece of paper be more powerful than this?
man says, to daughter,
          it's beautiful
man lies, but believes
it is true
wait let me start over

daughter says, to man,
          where did you get
          this pocket copy
          of the US constitution
man says, to daughter,
          they gave it to me
          when i became a citizen
daughter says, to man,
          they gave it to you for free?
man says, to daughter,
          being a citizen in this
          country is never free
man tells the truth
wait let me start over

nothing here is true
          except the sun
                    through the trees
          except the stories
                    that we're made of
& so
i eat my dinner
& so
i eat my history
& so
i become this world—a place to start over / not a blank canvas / not a forgetting
/ but a remembering / a story in perpetual motion / something that never stops
moving

is something that will never be
the same twice—
& so
i say, to anyone
who will listen,
i have never seen a day more beautiful than this one.

ODE TO THE TITANIUM SCREWS THAT HELD MY FIBULA TOGETHER FOR SIX MONTHS IN 2013

happy ten year anniversary
>to the time i broke my leg in two places and dislocated it from one.

happy ten year anniversary
>to laying on the sidewalk and not feeling anything from the sheer
>shock. happy ten year anniversary to numbness.

happy ten year anniversary
>to the ambulance arriving and my mom saying why did you call an
>ambulance, i could've carried you. happy twenty four and a half year
>anniversary to my mother giving birth to me after she carried
>me. happy twenty four and a half year anniversary to the last
>time i was carried so tenderly.

happy ten year anniversary
>to the me in the back of the ambulance realizing that my leg was broken
>because i could feel it. happy ten year anniversary to screaming and
>gritting my teeth and shutting my eyes and screaming and gritting my
>teeth and shutting my eyes and screaming and gritting my teeth and
>shutting my eyes. happy ten year anniversary to feeling myself in
>my body. happy ten year anniversary to asking for more morphine.
>happy ten year anniversary to not wanting to feel. happy ten year
>anniversary to my body, demanding to be felt.

happy ten year anniversary
>to the sleepless night before surgery in the morning, to not drinking
>water on the thirstiest day of my life, to waking up and forgetting that i
>had fallen asleep.

happy ten year anniversary
>to the last time i ran in the rain, slipped off a porch, and broke my leg.

happy ten year anniversary
>to taking my time, to tilting my head back to the deluge, to drinking it deep.

happy ten year anniversary
>to you're not going to feel a thing.

happy ten year anniversary
>to not feeling a thing, and instead feeling every thing.

happy ten year anniversary
>to the titanium screws they put in my leg.

happy nine and a half year anniversary
>to the removal of the titanium screws they put in my leg. happy nine and
>a half year anniversary to waking up from surgery and my mom telling me
>don't worry, she asked the nurse if we could take the screws home.

happy nine and a half year anniversary
        to my mom holding the titanium screws in her pink palm with nothing
        but exuberant joy & wonder to see what had come out of my body.
happy nine and a half year anniversary
        to waking up from surgery and blinking in the light.
happy nine and a half year anniversary
        to waking up.
happy one week anniversary
        to the last time it rained so hard i woke up feeling my ankle ache.
happy one day anniversary
        to waking up, and feeling.

warp & weft

i forgot you were queer
he says,
throwaway line from an unwritten
script picking lint off his shoulder i imagine
i am that sweater trying to fit against
a body that wants something i don't have
the language for

remember in this metaphor
    i am a sweater
    remember in this metaphor
        i am silent
        remember in this metaphor
            i don't know what language is so i don't wonder
            whether it is a gift or a burden

i forgot you were queer
he says i am that sweater those are his thumbs scraping
the lint of identity from the threads of my being

in weaving the two basic components are
the warp & the weft

the warp is longitudinal
held in tension across a loom

the weft is passed thru
& under

in my life i am held
in tension arms outstretched
absolute & ankles strained agony,
    don't you see, my joints are not alone
    dreaming of dislocation, all of me is
    eager to be somewhere else

in my life i am passed
thru & under by my own
hand, the weaver & the woven, wanting
only to fit against a body

in this conversation the expectations are pulled
taut across the doorframe, slicing me
to ribbons each time i pass thru

in this conversation the ribbons become knots
                              the knots become lies

in this conversation i am passed thru
& passed along
& passed around until
i am / passing

in my skin i have never
passed for white
my past predates me

in my sexuality i have to say it
again & again

in this history i am warped over
& over, until
i am twisted fragment of ribbon

in this language an intersection describes
two or more things that pass or lie across each other

in this context passing is the opposite
of *intersection*, is
separation,
        is tearing my parts,
                    apart

in this history passing is privilege
brings me closer to
        a whiter me
        a straighter me
        a me
                    that is
                            not me

in this language an *intersection* describes how something is divided
when something else is passing or
lying across it
in my self
          passing & lying / are one and the same
in my self
          i am
          the thing, divided, i am
          the thing, across it,
                    in my self
i am the warp i am the weft i am the intersection
                              & the whole world, intersecting

i forgot you were queer he says
                    &   i   forgot
to put on the sweater with
          all my names on it
& i forgot to let you pick
          the ones you
                    wanted to call me
& i forgot i was meant to rip
          myself apart
                    thread by thread
& i forgot i was supposed to lie
          across the loom
                    so i could be
unwoven

untitled craigslist post — snakes?

on the night the snakes came into the bed
they were black & tangled & wiry
& when i saw them out the corner of my eye i thought they were a pile of yarn
        as in i thought they were dreaming of being untangled
        as in i thought they were a reflection of the self
& when i saw them move i jumped
out of the bed   &   onto the floor,
        which was reassuring, in a way, in its firmness, its presence—
even as above the snakes writhed & swirled & coiled & uncoiled
                but it was that moment of movement that set me in motion

& the first thing i tried was standing up but my legs
were a little too weak for that

& the second thing i tried was foundering for my phone & thank
god i had dropped it out of bed with me

because the third thing i tried was googling "how to get snakes out of your bed"
& google said "did you mean *how to get **a snake** out of your bed?*"
& then my fear multiplied
tenfold, are you telling me no one's ever
experienced multiple snakes in the bed?
needless to say the results were sparse & unsatisfying,
& if i wanted a thing done right
i'd have to do it myself,   damn it,

& the fourth thing i tried was calling my friend because
if i wanted a thing done right
i'd have to do it myself,   damn it, but not alone, i'm scared to be alone,
& he said, "'s everything okay?"
        & i said "oh shit, were you sleeping?"
& he said, "well yeah, it's 2 AM,"
        & i said, "oh yeah. it's 2 AM,"
& he said, "you didn't know it was 2 AM, did you?"
        & i said "i knew,"
& neither of us believed me,

& he said, "dog, go to sleep," & then he fell asleep before i could even respond,
       & my response (had i responded) would have been "THERE
       ARE 14 SNAKES IN MY BED," which might've been an
       exaggeration but i'm bad at counting & good at exaggeration &
       i needed a response but i didn't need a response badly enough to
       wake him up, i'm not a monster, so instead i listened to the way
       his breathing sounded, soft & sleepy & slow, & i imagined that
       air in my own lungs, soft & sleepy & slow,

& the sixth thing i tried was standing up & my legs
could hold me this time

& when i stood up i saw there were like 5 snakes, max, which was way more
reasonable than the 14 that i had made up in my terrified state, but still enough
to keep me on my toes, because 5 snakes was still 4 more than the average
google search result,

& then i made eye contact with one of the snakes & that was the most terrifying
part of it all, i need you to know that,
       the rest of this story will get less terrifying from here on out,
but the moment that i stared at that snake, & that snake STARED BACK AT ME,
i forgot that i had a soul, or i remembered i had a soul
       (& i don't know which one was more terrifying),
finally it blinked or i blinked or the universe blinked I DON'T KNOW but
SOMEONE blinked
& that was enough for me
& it was like i was paul bunyan or paul rudd, whichever one of them was a
superhero, or pretended to be one, because i was pretending the fuck out of
being a superhero, & i hate pretending to be things i'm not, especially in my
own goddamn bedroom isn't that the one place i can stop pretending? but not
when there are five fucking snakes in the bed & i have to pretend i'm not afraid
of snakes
& i don't know how i did what i did next but fuck paul bunyan & fuck paul
rudd because neither of them has ever had to think about fiber arts, i'm sure, but
i did, in every single form,
knitting &   crocheting &   weaving &   sewing &
    quilting &   embroidering &,

because my mom is a quilter & her mom is a seamstress & i'm just me!,
         & none of us know how to keep our hands still
& my mom's hands
& her mom's hands
         & my hands were on the snakes
                  & the snakes were in my hands &
i know if my mom were there she would knit them into a sweater & my nani
would weave them into lace but all i can do is spin a damn good yarn

& by the end of it, they were tied together,
tail to tail to tail to tail to tail, teeth still
gnashing, tongues still
flickering, & i, woman still possessed, kept
tying & tying til the whole duvet was in knots
& i may have made something monstrous but at least i could call it mine

and i didn't know what to do with it after that, to be perfectly honest,
so i'm wondering,
does anyone know what to do with a bag of snakes? there's only 5,
which is too many for google to tell me reliably, i figure i'd ask here instead

self-possessed
after Sidney Gish's "Imposter Syndrome"

I am my own cat
I am hissing all the time and I have no idea why

I dash out the door and I don't know where I am
I am lost, almost always, and then I am merely outside

I can't remember how to knit,
I'm bad at roasting brussels sprouts,

I want to lay in the sun,
I'm always scaring myself in the dark, just with the mere truth of myself,

I'm looking & looking & looking
I'm closing my eyes & stretching

I'm shedding hair all over the goddamn floor
I don't want to vacuum

sorry,
I say to myself,
about the mess I made in the corner

and in response, I say,
oh, sweet baby it's an accident it happens to us all
or maybe I say,
stupid bitch bastard
yes i hate the landlord too, but who's going to clean that chaos

I am aching to be touched but no not like that and not like that and not like that
I don't want to be touched and if you touch me I will hiss, I swear

I will never drink the water I leave out for myself
I will chide myself for being dehydrated

my sandpaper tongue cuts to the bone
it says all sorts of things I can't possibly mean

I don't know how health insurance works
there are days where it is impossible to open the fridge

I still forgive myself
again and again and again

native speaker

this language is *laal*.
no this language is *chomona*.
no this language is *red*
red red bloody mouth. all
dying languages made prey
caught in the teeth. a prayer
before my lips could make
a sound. this language is red
as the tongue fleshy frightened
feeble the only muscle i know
how to flex & it can't carry
a damn thing except all this
history. when a language dies
the last words to go are the colors
when the lady on the bus tells me
she doesn't see color does she know
she is killing something between us? this language
is *red* laal chomona this language is *red* as
lineage: my mother's worry or my father's patience
or the words that can't describe either but we still

try. this language is dead like every day we destroy
it & make it something new this language
is *red* like the fire in which
it burned this language is *red* as rebirth
this language is spoken
it is not *read*

i am standing in the kitchen
with six native speakers
of gujarati & i find
none of them know
how to read & write the language
it doesn't exist anywhere in this home
except between our laughter &
behind our teeth

the day after the ten-year drought ended

nothing would dry
we hung towels on the back porch & we pressed freshly showered footprints
into the hardwood & we pulled the sheets out of the wash & we scrubbed the
countertops of the grit & grime & gorgonzola & we cleaned the blood between
our legs best we could & we pushed tears across the sodden wasteland of our
cheekbones & we couldn't see our reflections in the foggy mirror, much as we
tried & we felt the sweat drip down our necks & we remembered we had necks
& we watched condensation form & refuse to die & we watered the basil & it
nearly drowned & we opened our mouths & those jaws of starvation prayed for
salvation, or was it solvation, & we found flowers growing in the shower tiles, or
maybe it was black mold, but it grew nonetheless, life persists, & we sat under
the windowsill as the moon wept above & we understood for just one minute
why the sea has tides, why our tears disappear into thin air, why the puddles &
lakes & rivers & oceans evaporated overnight, & we understood, for just one
minute, why all water seeks to rise

in

Manchester	Cleveland	Lancaster
shouted	I	jumped
	transformed	
	into the	
Merrimack	Cuyahoga	Susquehanna
it heard me or it didn't but	it held all this history &	it forgave my self in its water
it swallowed my words the same	it still became new	
	when	
we built mills on your banks	industrial pollution caused	I say history I mean: the
we hoped to turn		Susquehanna River is the fifth
	the river	oldest river in the world: I mean
into capitalist production	to catch flame 50 years	is older than the Atlantic Ocean,
	ago we called it "necessary	& all our history
	consequence of prosperity"	
Merrimack made machine	Cuyahoga made chemical	Susquehanna made salvation

the river, thought we could
hold all this power in our

power in the water, yes, but all power
to the people, to the 1912 Lawrence
textile strike, to the immigrant workers
who didn't speak same **language** except
that of liberation

Merrimack made miracle

made new

all

imagining

finally

to capitalist **hell**scape forged by
our own

hands

called it river that doesn't
drown, but decays; Cleveland,
city that isn't **dying** but
begins again; post-**in**dustrial
apocalypse; nothing here but
our destiny

Cuyahoga made clean

all rivers are the same river

made new

this

imagine

what could

emerge

& young; I mean: the mountains
that cradle **our** river came after it,
came up around it, like

the water was warmer than i
thought it would be, closing over
my head, **rus**hing **in** to fill **the**
empty. **river** passes through my
fingers all the past i can't hold but
that still holds us

Susquehanna made story

made new

power

imagine

the start of a river

from a mouth

my grandfather was a terrorist
after Mosab Abu Toha

by which i mean / he was a watchmaker
lost in the ticking time bomb on the wrist of eternity
counting down seconds we don't share anymore

my grandfather was a terrorist
by which i mean / he taught me how to shuffle cards
without tucking an ace up the sleeve
without dropping even the lowest card
careful until the end

my grandfather was a terrorist
by which i mean / he wouldn't consider an outfit complete without a belt
he cared about the details
not for the devil
but for the divine

my grandfather was a terrorist
by which i mean / there's a photo of him holding a baby next to the Fox River &
when i saw the photo all i noticed was the way
he looked across the water
like he was dreaming
i was shocked when i noticed the baby, when i saw myself there, too,
i was shocked to find
that either of us were real

my grandfather was a terrorist
by which i mean / he was a muslim man in countries that wanted him dead
& this is an ode to muslim men everywhere
but i'm not the best at formal poetry
so forgive me
if this is an elegy instead
forgive me if your life is defined by nothing more
than your death

i never knew the word terror
so long as i loved you
until the day
the phone rang
& they told me
you were dead.

Wendy's chili finger lady comes clean

y'all heard about this? she confessed

lady goes to wendy's & tells everyone she found a finger in the chili
turns out it's not the finger of anyone employed by wendy's
she admitted that she got the finger off her husband
turns out it's not her husband's finger either
he admitted that he got the finger off his coworker

turns out he lost it in an industrial accident
& just held onto it after

lady & husband paid him $100 for the finger
i can't blame the coworker,
i'll be the first to admit that i've held onto a part of myself longer than i
should, that i'd jump at the chance to get my body away from my body

i can't blame the lady, either
who wouldn't run an elaborate scheme at wendy's
in the hopes of getting free chili for life?

when i'm in the club asking ladies for their digits,
THIS IS WHAT I MEAN!!
when i say i need someone to finger me right now,
THIS IS WHAT I'M TALKING ABOUT!!
i'm not even asking for your hand, just the tip!!

who wouldn't run an elaborate scheme at wendy's
in the hopes of getting free chili for life
i would, once

because eating chili in the drive thru tastes like memory
like knowing my mom wants nothing more than a hot meal
for once not made by her hands

she didn't have to put her blood sweat & tears anywhere in the drive thru
she didn't have to be everything she could just be alive, & that was enough

i haven't had wendy's in years
& probably won't again

my memory stays in my memory
my mom's blood sweat & tears is all over me, makes both of us alive

i don't want wendy's free chili for life anymore that's just the blood sweat
& tears of strangers trying to
live and getting exploited instead
i want that place brought to its knees

so if anyone has a spare finger laying around i'd love to see it
& moreover the only industrial accident i'm interested in
is accidentally causing the downfall of a fast food industry
with nothing but a prayer from our palms

ok i've written myself into a corner i think
how is this poem going to be about picking up ladies & crime & boycotting
wendy's & my MOM—i already know—it's in the title
let me come clean
the proof isn't in the pudding
it's in the goddamn crockpot
slow cooking for hours or centuries they feel the same anyway
warmed with our fiery love & righteous anger they feel the same anyway
& all you have to do is want / to start a fire / with your own hands

every immigrant mom i know hates siri

they can't stand the idea of a disembodied female voice telling them what to do / when i ask Gertie Aunty why she feels this way / she says / i already have my mother-in-law for that

i think of my mom's mom standing over open flame proving herself with a hot meal / fingertips on cast iron / fingerprints long gone / i think of her mother-in-law's voice / bemused & smug & judgment / as though this woman at the stove was not good enough for her son / i think of my mom saying she was married to my dad for years before his parents liked her / i think of my mom, origin of my people pleaser complex, / i think of years & years & years & years / i think of a world where family means everything / so the barrier to entry is a million miles high / it requires you to lose every part of yourself / to rip yourself to pieces & throw them across the globe

my mom used to argue with the gps lady / used to say / what's wrong with a map, i can tell you directions too, & she could, highways gathering like synapses, fingers steepling under the chin, all i've ever known is how to get lost & in that losing at least i can know family is that which / makes the map smaller / i'm sure of it / as i'm sure that i left my heart in san francisco & i left my prefrontal cortex in cleveland, ohio & i left my pinky toenail in the rocky mountains & i left my superego in the woods, somewhere & i wonder if that means i'm less of a whole or more of it / that the world rushes in to connect me across continents / do not imagine a left kidney in the grand canyon / instead imagine phantom ligaments stretching across the map / my body / bigger than the mercator projection / no longer a mind-body problem because of course they're connected / it would be impossible to have it any other way

when you say family means everything / i imagine instead a world where family means everything so / EVERYTHING / means / family: the sun through the window on a tuesday afternoon / the spinach stuck in your teeth / the honest feedback that there's spinach stuck in your teeth / the pizza hut large pizza special / the cast iron skillet that never burned our fingers / the disagreement over what to have for dinner / the disagreement, yes that's family too / the forgetting / the remembering / the leaving / even the leaving / even when you don't have a map
i imagine a world where family is this world
overflowing from our hands
& we don't know where to put it / we've never known where to put it so instead we put it / in each other's hearts

ancestral cursing

my father and i have different swear words
like when i say
fuck   i mean fuck
but when he says fuck
         slamming on the brakes / cut off in traffic / my first time hearing this word
         i, seven years old, say
         what does that word mean & he says
                  that   is a word   that makes   birds fall
                                                                 from the heavens

my father and i have different swear words
but the same delusions
of grandeur

like when i say
shit   i mean swearing
can reduce our perception of pain
but when he says
ouch   he means ouch
i've heard him lie / but i've never heard him say shit
like when he says
LANGUAGE   he means you're this close
to washing your mouth with soap

like when i say
damn   i mean we are all condemned to our fates
like when i say damn / he says bloody hell
& when he says
bloody hell   he means
         his parents grew up in british india   he means
         british bastard   border builder   birthplace breaker
         he means   this imperialism is nothing
         except open wound on the subcontinent
         he means   the british spilled blood   enough
               on this earth   it could douse the flames of hell
         he means   the 1888 Oxford English Dictionary comments
               the word bloody is   very vulgar & is now
               constantly in the mouths of the lower classes

he means   the colonizer can pretend
        all they like but their mouths are no cleaner
        than ours he means   bloody hell. we aren't fated
        to burn in hell. hell isn't fated to burn.
        it's fated to bleed.
        he means
                our fates are as fluid as we are

like when i say william and kate are coming to boston / he says great,
go to the event, and take a sign that says
        RETURN THE CROWN JEWELS BILLY
that means   when the british empire bleeds
its rubies run rivulets for the rest of us

like when i say
i swear   it's the truth
he says all stories   are about lying
like when i say
shit   i mean language helps us heal
even when it's a lie
like when i say
language   i mean yeah, the colonizer's tongue
it can
choke them
the same

when we say nothing
we mean everything

& when this word has power
        it's because we make it so

& when this language curses you
to act / it's because
the fucking birds
will fall   from the sky
if you don't

STEAL THIS POEM

break it into a million pieces
here's a line about love
& another one about loss
& here's one about love and loss just to remember
they never exist without each other

here's an anecdote
yes, steal this too
let it be a story
let you tell it with a glint
in your eye that looks
like a reflection, or a star:

i have seen my mom
cross state lines &
international borders &
stand next to bodies of water &
every time without fail she will see
a cool rock and pick it up & say look
at this rock, & she'll hold it
in her palm & collect more & more til they ring
against each other like bells each trying
to be heard and my dad will see this little treasure and say
no way we're taking these home
they're just dead weight
they're just rocks & here's a nice little metaphor
take this one with you: we take the rocks home every time
how could we not how could a border
ever stand in the way of a really cool rock
how could the dead Wait? they've already
left how could we have a home
any other way how could we pretend
our lives we've made aren't just the holding
onto each other, trying to be heard

when you rip this poem apart
scatter it to the wind
stanzas catching in the sunlight
syllables crashing into the sea

let this line drift away
let this one wash to shore
let it sink into a pocket, somewhere,
& still make a sound

57

recency bias
after Zeke Russell

recency bias but not the bad kind. recency bias like you just went home for the night & i already want you to come back. recency bias like we've been laughing for so long i forget what we were laughing about. recency bias like i remember & it doesn't hurt. recency bias like i refuse to forget. recency bias like i will forget i know i will & when i do it will be okay. the happening was enough. i was changed by the circumstances even if i can't remember them. recency bias like short term memory loss like i'm living in the present even as i am acting out my past & imagining my future. recency bias like i have never known anything but the now. recency bias like time isn't real like the only thing separating us is the sound of the door closing. recency bias like i can't tell if the key is turning in the lock to shut it or / to open

language immersion

no i'm not the most anxious woman alive because my mom hasn't died yet
her native language is worrying and she taught it to me well
when i consider mother tongue
i don't think of gujarati ancestral dialect my mom didn't pass on but
rather *what did you have for dinner* or
i missed your call is everything okay or
have you been using that foot cream i gave you
when i remember her voice
it's the colonizer's tongue
but it's all her fury her joy her wonder her worry

when she sings in the kitchen
she hums she murmurs she croons
there are no words here

when i worry about my beloveds
it's because love & loss are two sides
of the same coin. you can't have one
without the other. you can't have an ending
without the beginning—

when my mom asks me why
all my poems are about her dying
i don't have a good answer which is
maybe yet another reason i'm killing her slowly

when i confess to her my fear
that when she ages she will forget
english and speak solely in gujarati,
she tells me oh yeah, that could happen

there is no way to talk about life without talking about death
there is no way for me to talk without her
& all the words she gave me
& all the worry she gave me
there is no language that reaches
past that future through that grief

there is no way for me to talk about my life without talking about my mother's
she brought me into this world
only she can take me out
everyone else can try their damnedest but
i won't die until she does
& even then, her life in mine
her heart in my chest
her voice in my head
singing in this home
keeping the silence at bay

**last week we asked taizoon mamu what the name taizoon meant
    & he said**

last week we asked taizoon mamu what the name taizoon meant & he said
one you bow down to every time you see them
which was just so funny

something about the weight of the delivery
sounded both so ironic and so genuine

like even if he was making it up
it was enough meaning to make new

identity / so let me make myself joke
not pronounced punchline / but spoken

like fresh way to discover the truth
with laughter behind the teeth

the next time someone asks me
what my name means i have half a mind to tell them

it means / fuck off / or it means / do i look like an encyclopedia / or it means
/ what does your name mean, Barbara? so exotic! / or it means / one you bow
down to every time you see them / or it means / enough gravity to draw us back
to the earth / or it means / seeing syllables & knowing someone exists in the gap
between them / or it means / laughter behind the teeth / or it means / do you
get it? / or /

my name is aparna.
i don't have the words
for it yet but i think / it means:

Acknowledgments

All my thanks to the places where these poems first appeared:
—"the day after the ten-year drought ended" in DMQ Review (Summer 2023)
— "thought to be one of the rarest snakes in north america, no louisiana pine snake has been seen in the last decade, until today, when we start to see them everywhere" in GOOD SOUP (vol. 1, 2024)
— "untitled craigslist post - snakes?" in the engine(idling (vol. 6, May 2025)
— "these days, everybody wants to hear the prophecies of yore at a mcdonald's drive thru, and i just don't think that's what i'm after" in Voicemail Poems (Fall 2025)

First and foremost my family: Mom, Dad, Amar. Thank you for teaching me the importance of sharing a meal together and laughing together at the dinner table. I love you beyond words. Thank you to Nani, Nana, Appachayan, Ammachi. To Yusuf Uncle & Shaheen Aunty & the many times I've felt at home in your house. To all my family between here & India, to all the aunties & uncles, whether we're related or not, family or family friends or cousins or whatever word aspires to describe the indescribable. Honorable mention to Yosi Uncle who, when I told him I was writing a book of poems, immediately responded, "'How can I be lost / if I've got nowhere to go?' Metallica. That's poetry," which is coincidentally the thesis of this collection and also does what our beloveds do best: keep us humble in a way that pushes us forward.

Thank you so much to my editor, slam team coach, and friend Myles Taylor. Thank you for everything, but especially thank you for the time you gently told me "YOUR POEMS MAKE PEOPLE UNCOMFORTABLE," for reminding me and encouraging me to take up space. Thank you to the whole team at Game Over Books, especially Josh Savory for seeing a spark in this manuscript in its earliest days and Catherine Weiss for the incredible cover design.

Thank you to everyone involved in the artwork, printing, & musical performances of my first two chapbooks: Mimi Shalf, Areeb Ahmed, Madi Ebersole, Mara Tu, Nadim Najjar, Nico Tapiero, Rahul Brito, Rhea Lamba, Winston Liao, Yukai Tomsovic, & the bands Spiderwater, Lemon in the Weed Pipe, and Where's Waldo Audiobook. Thank you for making art with me but more importantly thank you for your friendship. Honorable mention to Mimi Shalf, for weird art and for teaching me the importance of some really good soup.

For Alex Welsh, Andy Halza, & Jenni Marer, who were some of the earliest and most enthusiastic readers of my poetry. For Ammar Abidi, the first person to buy anything I publish and the most responsibly chaotic baker I know. For Aashna Shah, my earliest partner in themed house parties. For Katy Shenk, Luke Schaffer, & Madi Ebersole for cheesecake in the parking lot.

Thank you to all my friends without whom I could not live this joyous & wondrous life that breathes in all my work. Honorable mention to Areeb Ahmed, who once asked me what a friend was, & to which I still have not a single answer but luckily many, many, many examples.

Thank you to the Elizabethtown Public Library, and every library, for being the site of every story & salve to every curious mind. To my teachers who taught me to read carefully & question everything: Ms. Piede, Ms. Bradley, Mr. Safford, Dr. Vrettos, Professor Grimm. To my first poetry teacher, Thom Dawkins, and every poet I've met since then. Thank you to Matt, Michelle, Ryan, & Nahomy at Literary Cleveland for showing me what a literary community can be.

The words thank you are not big enough for everyone who has ever passed through the Cantab Lounge on a Wednesday night. Thank you to Dawn Gabriel & Myles Taylor for restarting the Boston Poetry Slam in 2022 & thank you to any regular, feature, or first-time poet who has touched the stage there. Thank you to all the poets with whom I've been on a BPS team. Thank you to Northbeast and the New England poetry scene. Thank you to: Alex Kist, Amy Argentar, Anthony Febo, Arielle Gray, Briana Crockett, Brynna Boyd, Crystal Valentine, Disha Trivedi, Ed Wilkinson, Emmanuel Oppong-Yeboah, Ilse Ruizvosfocri, Ilyus Evander, Jennifer Martinez, Jess Rizkallah, Jimmy Pavlick, Joshua Nguyen, Kai Wallins, Kaitie Dilán, Kat Anderson, Katya Zinn, Kenny Bradley, Kris Cho, Lip Manegio, Logan Lopez, March Penn, Mckendy Fils-Aimé, ML, Otto Vock, Ren L[i]u, Ryan Phung, Sam Cha, Sara H, Will Leonard, Youssef Mohamed, Zeke Russell, & all the poets I missed but whose words have changed me forever. Thank you for your work.

These poems would not exist without all your voices in my head. This collection would not exist without all your hands holding me together. Honorable mention to Zoya: when I told her the Boston Poetry Slam is every Wednesday, she responded "poetry is…forever?" It is as forever as any of us are. Thank you dear reader for bearing witness to & joining me on this little eternity. Thank you for holding these poems in your hands & head & heart. Thank you for meeting me here.

Notes

EVERYONE LOVES A PARTY is after "Variations on a Theme by Elizabeth Bishop" by John Murillo.

The conversation in **these days, everybody wants to hear the prophecies of yore at a mcdonald's drive thru, and i just don't think that's what i'm after** never happened but could not have existed without my friendship with Luke Schaffer. When I called him to read him the poem, he said "Wow, a poem can just be a series of intrusive thoughts?"

i spell my name began in a workshop taught by Myles Taylor.

The movie quoted in **i don't remember the movie but in it a character says** is Avatar: Way of Water (2022).

thought to be one of the rarest snakes in north america, no louisiana pine snake has been seen in the last decade, until today, when we start to see them everywhere echoes a line by Nico Tapiero, which is "it hurts so much / to fall back into ourselves."

ekphrasis after the moderated panel on the exhibition Please Stay Home at Harvard's Carpenter Center, free to all, featuring the work of Darrel Ellis, who died of AIDS in 1992 includes quotes from the panelists Leslie Hewitt, Wardell Milan, Robert F. Reid-Pharr, and Makeda Best.

man lies began in a workshop taught by Sam Cha.

self-possessed is after the opening lines of the song "Impostor Syndrome" by Sidney Gish. The lines are "Unfortunately, I am / My own dog."

In **native speaker,** the fact about "when a language dies / the last words to go are the colors" is from the article "Should a Country Speak a Single Language?" by Samanth Subramanian, published in The New Yorker (November 2024).

my grandfather was a terrorist is after Mosab Abu Toha's poem of the same name.

a water-powered textile mill turns rushing rivers into cloth draws from and quotes the article "Cuyahoga River Fire" by Michael Rotman, published by Cleveland Historical (2010).

Wendy's chili finger lady comes clean takes its title & establishing information from the article "Wendy's 'Chili Finger Lady' Comes Clean" by Jessica Greene published by NBC Bay Area (2010).

every immigrant mom i know hates siri quotes Gertie Castillo.

ancestral cursing quotes the Oxford English Dictionary, vol. 1 (1888).

STEAL THIS POEM is loosely after "If I Must Die" by Refaat Alareer.

recency bias is after the line "all we have is the now" by Zeke Russell.

last week we asked taizoon mamu what the name taizoon meant & he said quotes Taizoon Jhaveri.

Biography

Aparna Paul (she/her) is a writer, chemical engineer, banana bread enthusiast, & amateur crossword constructor based in Cambridge, MA. Her poetry & prose has been recognized by *Reckoning*, *DMQ Review*, & Gaining Ground, among others. She edited the anthology Reflections of The Land (Literary Cleveland, 2022) and is a co-editor of *GOOD SOUP*, now on hiatus (@goodsoup.mag on insta!). She performs regularly, hosts occasionally, and slams sometimes at the Boston Poetry Slam at the Cantab Lounge. *HOME FREE* (Game Over Books, 2025) is her debut full-length poetry collection.

I Could Die Today and Live Again | Summer Farah

Summer Farah's latest chapbook redefines the pop culture poem, linking Palestine to the Legend of Zelda, immigration to dying and living again. These poems call on literary ancestors like Etel Adnan and lyricist Mitski to reframe and recharacterize diaspora, longing, and the double-headed hydra of diaspora.

Masculinity Parable | Myles Taylor

Boston slam poetry legend Myles Taylor comes forth with a debut collection like a proverb. These poems celebrate queer joy and resistance in the face of societal pressures of conformity. In these rhythmic verses, Taylor brings forth the myth of gender presentation, and holds trans masculinity as a parable—a harbinger for a future of freedom.

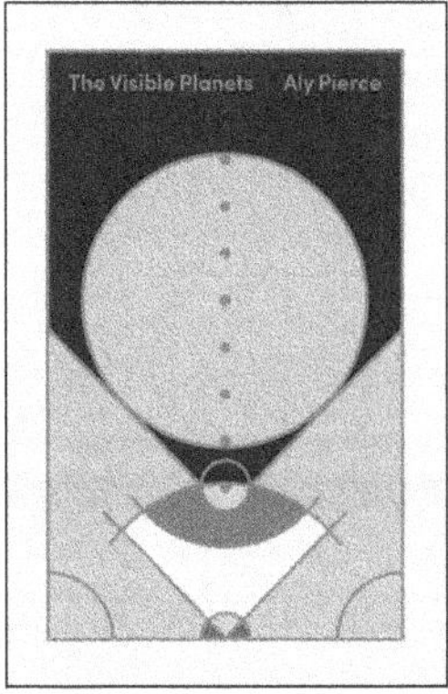

The Visible Planets | Aly Pierce

Aly Pierce's poetry places planets and stars in conversation with human life. Straddling the border between science and art, Pierce brings astronomy to life, tying in legends from astrological tales and Roman myths and mirroring them against the mundanity of real life. What if Saturn sat at the dinner table? What if we were Callisto? What keeps us apart from the skies?

www.gameoverbooks.com